LANCASHIRE BONDS

Another Saturday Evening at
The Duck and Trumpet, Oswaldtwistle

by

Alan and Les Bond

Landy Publishing
1999

ISBN 1 872895 48 4

British Library in Cataloguing Publication Data.
A catalogue record of this book is available from the British Library.

Layout by Mike Clarke. *Tel/Fax: 01254 395848*
Printed by Nayler the Printer Ltd., Accrington. *Tel: 01254 234247*

Landy Publishing have also published:

Lancashire Lingo Lines; dialect poetry edited by Bob Dobson
Lancashire, this, that an't'other by Doris Snape
Lancashire Laugh Lines by Kay Davenport
Accrington Observed by Brian Brindle & Bob Dobson
Accrington's Changing Face by Frank Watson & Bob Dobson
An Accrington Mixture edited by Bob Dobson
Blackburn in Times Gone By by Jim Halsall
Blackburn Tram Rides by Jim Halsall
A Blackburn Miscellany edited by Bob Dobson
Blackburn's West End by Matthew Cole
Blackburn's Shops at the Turn of the Century by Matthew Cole
Blackburn and Darwen a Century Ago by Alan Duckworth
Clitheroe Ablaze with Glory by Sue Holden
Sand Grown: the story of Lytham St. Annes by Kathleen Eyre
Rishton Remembered by Kathleen Broderick
Wrigley's Writings; Songs and Monologues by Bernard Wrigley

A full list is available from:

Landy Publishing
'Acorns' 3 Staining Rise, Staining, Blackpool, FY3 0BU
Tel/Fax: 01253 895678

CONTENTS.

A Word in Thi Ear

Amongst the various definitions of '*bond*' is that which means two things being joined together to become as one. My brother, '*eawr Alan*', and I were Bonds who had such a bond, and felt bonded to Lancashire, the county which leads the way.

Alan was five years older than me. He died in 1992, but whilst he was alive, he and I shared a special brotherly relationship. If either of us got kicked, t' other limped.

We shared many things from our earliest days playing out in clogs as lads in Accrington; the love of Lancashire, its humour, its history, its musical traditions and the telling of tales in verses and prose. We shared the writing of poems, sitting down at a table, often in a bar, and scribbling out our individual ideas towards a common end. Even now, if I write a poem, I declare it as being written by the pair of us.

Whenever Alan 'took the stage' he explained that what was to follow was "*a perfectly true story*". This meant just the opposite. I'm one for honest truth in the word-pictures I paint. Call me simple and owd-fashioned if you like.

In 1981, we published a collection of thirteen of our poems in a 40-page booklet entitled ***Extracts from Saturday Evening at the Duck and Trumpet, Oswaldtwistle***. Some people thought that the ***Duck and Trumpet*** didn't exist and that the Saturday literary evenings were a product of our imagination, perhaps brought on by drinking too much of the Lollard's Best Bitter available there. Many sought out the pub after enjoying our poems, so this is a second helping for them, and a first course for everyone else. Everyone is invited to the Real Ales and Real Tales venue on the first Saturday in every month, especially those who will get up onto their feet and perform a monologue.

Towards the end of the book I've included a few poems written in recent years for the annual Lancashire Fire Brigade Safety Week. In them you'll meet Billy Myres *who's allus 'avin chip pan fires*. I've also included lines written by Mally Dow, Jim Atherton, Dave Dutton and Keith Scowcroft when they learned of Alan's death. I thank them for their permission to use their work. I also thank David Caffrey, Julian Davies and Barbara Blundell for the drawings which embellish the book.

Les Bond
August 1999.

Alan, pint in hand, and Les enjoying a get-together just before Alan's untimely death.

THE LONE RANGER

T' Lone Ranger were ridin' through Blackburn,
Wi' Tonto, his Indian mate.
T' Lone Ranger said, "*Does ta fancy a pint?*"
Tonto said, "*That would be great, Kee mo sabbi.*"

So they pulled up outside t' **Duck and Trumpet**,
And hitched up their hosses to t' rail.
Lone Ranger ordered a glass of best mild,
And Tonto a glass of brown ale.

Now t' landlord o' t' pub, he were biased
Against folk wi' a bit darker skin.
In fact, if you lived south of Bolton
You'd be banned and you wouldn't get in.

So when he looked up and saw Tonto,
His nostrils flared open wide.
He then pulled a pint for t' Lone Ranger
And told Tonto, "*Thee get outside.*"

Now outside o' t' pub, it were snowin'
And blowing a cold icy breeze.
"*He can't wait out theer*", said Lone Ranger,
"*It's cowd, an' he'll flamin' well freeze.*"

But Tonto knew just what the score was,
And he said as he'd come to no harm,
If he put on his pumps an' his muffler,
And ran round outside to keep warm.

Two hours and twenty pints later,
After four bags of crisps and a pie,
T' Lone Ranger slid off his bar stool,
Slumped onto t' floor, there to lie.

In through the door rushed Owd 'Arry.
"*Is t' Lone Ranger in here?*" he cried.
"*Someone should tell him, when he comes to,
His Injun's still running, outside.*"

THE KING'S VISIT TO HOGHTON TOWER

On a parky, wet mooarnin' in Howt'n,
  It wer foggy so yo' wouldn't see,
A powfagged owd Pooastmon coom puffin' up t' brew.
  "I've a letter fray t' King 'ere fer thee."

He wer speykin' to Richard de Howt'n,
  Who wer caherin' at t' dooer, in 'is vest.
  "Sitha, tha piecan," sez Richard,
  "Ah'm owt bar in t' mood fer a jest."

Pooastmon gi' Dickie a parchment,
  Sayin', *"Sken at yon King's Royal Seal."*
Then biddin' a gradely, *"Good morrow."*
  He slithert reawnd, slow on 'is 'eel.

Dickie wer lollin' on t' jobestooan,
  When 'is een oppen'd wide wi' deleet,
Cus 'e read as King James, who wer traipsin' through Preston,
  Wer coomin' to Dick's to stop t' neet.

Neaw t' drahvway as led up to Dick's place,
  Wer pot'oyled an' sluchy an' wet.
  E'd a liked ta 'ave 'ed id Macadamed.
  But id edn'd bin invented just yet.

So 'e sloped off to t' mon as sowd carpets,
  Who greeted Sir Dick wi' a smile,
Thad grew wider when 'e fun as carpet 'e wanted,
  Ud measure t' best part on a mile.

Thi reawled t' carpet eawt, deawn Dick's drahvway,
  And waited fer t' King to appear.
He, at last, traycled up in a carriage,
  An sez to Sir Richard - *"Ah'm 'ere."*

Then 'e lucked up an si t' carpet,
  An then sez to Dick - so wer towd,
  *"Reyt gradely owd lad, wod a welcum,
  Owd fettler, tha's done mi reyt prowd."*

Thi piked off up drahve o' thur chargers,
An' th' 'osses fillt carpet wi' nast.
But a mon swept aw t' coddy muck up fer 'is rhubob,
When aw th' 'angers-on 'ad geet past.

When neet time ad fawen o'er t' Tower,
Jem sez ta Dick, *"What's fer t' tay?
I think tha shud gi' mi a party".*
"Reyt Sire," said Dick, *"Straight away."*

He wer eytin' some beeaf when id 'appened,
An' chompin' 'is choppers on t' booan,
An' cobbin' t' remains o'er 'is showder,
To a dog as 'ed punced under t' throoan.

*"This beeaf is t' best as Ah've etten,
Id licks t' others cleyn eawt o' sight."*
An' 'e pooed eawt 'is soowerd an' bashed it,
An' turned beeaf, thad day, into knight.

Then 'e carried on eytin' an' suppin'
Till 'e keyked o'er, an' fell off 'is stoo'.
He said, *"Nowt licks an 'Owt'n Tower welcome,
Ah've 'ed a reyt good Lancashire do."*

T' King started wi' veal, pullets, tripe an' ceaw 'eel,
Pigeons, black puddin' an' mustard,
Pheasant and quail, a quart o' strong ale,
An a gurt piece o' bunnock an' custard.

Then t' party geet goin' an' th' ale started flowin',
An Jem danced as best 'e wer able,
Till Dick shouted out, *"Supper's ready."*
An t' King med a mad dash back to t' table.

THE MYSTERY OF THE *MARIE CELESTE*

There are stories of swift racing horses,
And dogs that run faster than sound,
But I know of a wonderful creature,
A creature of skill and renown.
It's Sammy; the world famous woodworm,
Whose deed is in history wrote down.

One day Sammy was feeling quite poorly,
And a trip on the sea was advised.
So he took the first train down to Plymouth,
Where those great wooden ships he espied,
And the sight of those ships
Made him lick both his lips.
"I'm spoiled for choice", Sammy cried!

He looked at them all with excitement,
Then chose one called *Marie Celeste*.
She was loaded with cargoes of timbers,
So he knew that this choice was the best.
And he squealed with delight
When he took his first bite,
And he swore then he'd eat all the rest.

Four times a day little Sammy
Would paddle his feet in the sea,
Each time was from somewhere quite different
After breakfast, lunch, dinner and tea,
He'd chew a big hole in the ship's wooden wall,
What a hungry young woodworm was he!

Black 'Arry, the boat's one-eyed joiner,
Was inspecting the ship's wooden keel,
He'd just copped an eyeful the previous day,
When all was a watertight seal.
What he saw made him flinch,
There were holes every inch,
And he swore it was the sea he could feel.

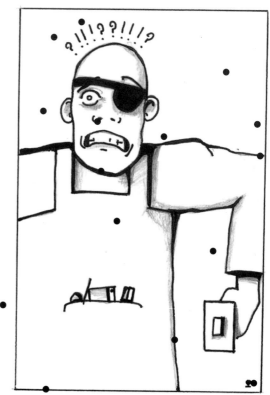

So he rushed up to speak to the captain,
 To tell him that all was not well.
But the captain was playing Monopoly,
With a woman called 'Big Busted Nell'.
 When he told him, he laughed,
 And said *"Don't talk so daft,*
 This ship is sound as a bell".

Making dinner, the cook a week later,
 Realised that his feet were all wet.
He thought all his spuds had boiled over,
 Whilst checking the table was set.
 So turning to switch off the oven,
A great cauldron of porridge he spilled,
And the porridge sunk down through the water,
Then down through the floorboards it swilled.

As the captain jumped into the lifeboat,
 The crew enquired what was amiss.
The sight of the hold filling slowly with water,
 Made the mate shout, *"I don't fancy this"*.
 The crew then made a mad scramble,
 And into the lifeboat they fled,
Just as Sammy was sampling its tiller,
 And thinking of going to bed.

Within three days the lifeboat was finished,
 Like a sieve it sunk under the waves.
Alas! That was the end of poor Sammy,
And the crew went down too - none were saved.
But the porridge that sunk through the floorboards,
 Sealed all the holes Sammy made,
 And the water all *E-VAP-OR-A-TED*,
 So on top of the sea the ship stayed.

Now you know the truth of the story,
 That has baffled the experts for years,
And if sympathy you're feeling for Sammy,
 Don't feel bad if you shed a few tears.
 'Cos Sammy's deed lives on for ever,
For on board ships from Shanghai to Brest,
 At night sailors speak in low whispers
 Of the mystery of the *Marie Celeste*.

9

RUDOLPH'S DRUNKEN BLUNDER

I wer' standing in t' *Duck and Trumpet*,
Enjoying a nice early drink.
Big Brenda, Cross-eyed Mick's wife,
Wer' washing some glasses in t' sink.

When in came a bright breezy stranger,
Man of swift wit and fast repartee.
Big Brenda kept him waiting at t' bar,
Till he shouted, *"Hey, come and serve me."*

*"A pint of best mild and some peanuts
and tickle your bum with a feather."*
Big Brenda whipped round and said, *"What did you say?"*
He said, *"Typical Belthorn weather."*

She served him his pint and his peanuts;
On her face was a vague puzzled look.
She went back to the sink, undecided;
Not sure whether she'd been mistook.

Rudolph was sat there in t' corner,
He wer drunk; he'd been drinking all day.
He said, *"I heard what you said to Big Brenda.
Will you tell me again what to say?"*

*"Well, you order a pint, or whatever you want,
And say, 'Tickle your bum with a feather',
And when they ask you to repeat what you said,
Tell 'em, 'Typical Belthorn weather'."*

Now, Rudolph thought he'd like to try it,
But Brenda had gone for her tea,
And Mick had come into the bar to serve,
He were standing there talking to me.

The stranger drank all of his beer up,
Wiped the froth from his mouth and then smiled,
Pushed his beer glass over to Rudolph and said,
"You try it now - mine's mild."

"Two pints o' mild, Mick", slurred Rudolph,
"And shove a feather up your a**e", he said.
Mick shot straight, bolt, upright,
And I felt myself going red.

'Cos Mick hasn't much sense of humour.
"What - did - you - say?" he cried.
Rudolph giggled and winked and said,
"It's p***ing down, outside."

This page has kindly been sponsored by Cross-eyed Mick, long time licensee of the **Duck and Trumpet**, Thyckear St., Oswaldtwistle. Keeper of the best pint of Lollard's Fine Beers and Ales as featured in the Church, Oswaldtwistle and Knuzden Best Beer Guide since 1906.

THE UNKINDEST CUT OF ALL
(OUCH)

Rudoplph came home late one evening,
He wer drunk, he'd been drinkin' all day.
His wife, she wer peylin' potatoes,
Makin' some chips fer their tay.

He slurred through his inebriation,
"Come on love, give me a kiss."
She said, *"If I'd listened to mother.
She said you'd end up just like this."*

Her anger made Rudolph excited.
He determined that he'd have it off.
He advanced, in his hand was his person,
But she said, *"NO! I'll have it off!"*

She picked up the knife from the table,
And brought it down hard, with a thump.
Away went one half of his manhood,
He was left with a thirteen inch stump.

The Judge said, *"You evil woman,
Can you not see what you've done?
No more can he boast like a fisherman,
Now only with finger and thumb."*

He ordered her to keep the peace,
But she was all in a fog.
*"I'm sorry M'lud, I can't keep the piece,
'Cos I've fed the piece--- to the dog."*

THE KINDHEARTED BOOKMAKER

One day, as I walked past a bookmaker's shop,
Something I saw made me falter and stop.
A man with clothes that were shabby and worn,
Stood in the doorway looking forlorn,
His eyes all welled up and he started to cry.
I asked him his problem, he gave this reply.
He said he had been in the 'bookies' all day,
And lost all his social security pay.
He then started kicking the bookmaker's door,
'Til the sole of one shoe half fell off on the floor.
Just then the bookie drove up in his Rolls,
And looked at the man with the semi-detached soles.
From out of his pocket he drew a big wad,
And said he would help this unfortunate 'bod'.
He casually rolled off the e-lastic band
And stood there with all the loose notes in his hand.
He gave him the elastic and these words I heard,
"This will hold on your soles 'til you get them repaired."

All proceeds from this page will be donated to the
Destitute Bookmakers' Benevolent Fund.

11

THE LANDLORD'S REVENGE

I'll tell thee a tale of a trickster,
Arnold Craggot is his name.
He's a mon to beware of,
'Cos practical jokes are his game.

No one has shook hands wi' Arnold for years,
For he gives you an e-lectric shock,
And hundreds of teeth have been broke on brush handles,
Painted to look just like rock.

If he gives thee a fag, it blows up in your face,
And many's the pub where he's banned
For putting match heads into t' darts marker's chalk,
So it flares up and burns all his hand.

He once emptied t' pub in three seconds
When he came in and let loose a snake.
We all scrambled out, except Kershaw,
Who were drunk and thought t' snake were a fake.

What did it were t' two-sided sucker
That caused a hell of a fray.
'Cos Rudolph, who wer' sat theer in t' corner,
Wer' drunk; he'd been drinkin' all day.

He stuck Rudolph's pint to the top of the bar.
Poor Rudolph who wer' nissed as a pewt,
Wrestled his beer up, to drink it
And threw it all o'er t' landlord's suit.

That wer' t' last straw for the landlord
Who'd put up with his tricks far too long.
He devised a good way to get even,
And decided, this time, he'd do Craggot some wrong.

Now! In t' backyard o' t' pub lives Brutus,
A dog as stands near six foot tall.
Guarding the landlord's possessions
Fro' robbers who'd climb o'er t' back wall.

But the trouble is, wi' this flockhound,
In t' backyard he's left to roam free.
And t' toilets are out there in t' corner,
And he won't let you out for a pee.

But you follow a laid down procedure,
If you want to go out to the stones,
You whisper in t' landlady's ear'ole,
And she gives you a couple of bones.

Then! you fearlessly stride to the doorway,
And sling a bone right down the yard,
And whilst Brutus chases this morsel,
You run t' toilet, while he's off guard.

But Brutus is quite a fast eater,
And he's very soon after some more.
So you sling t' second bone into t' corner,
And make a dash back to the door.

So with cunning and secret connivance,
T' landlord brewed strong sennapod beer,
And kept it there, just under t' counter,
Then waited for him to appear.

On the stroke of twenty and a half minutes past seven,
Arnold appeared with a grin,
Sporting a new squirty flower in his button hole,
And a blooming great spring in a tin.

T' landlord wer' flushed with excitement,
'Cause he knew this was his finest hour,
He knew that tonight he would taste sweet revenge.
So he even smelled Arnold's new flower.

Then! From under the counter he brought it,
Saying, *"This one is special for you.*
I'd like to get expert opinion,
On this highly original brew."

Arnold, at first, had a tentative sniff,
Then guzzled it down wi' no bother.
And smacking his lips, he said, *"Boy that wer' good.*
I'd be pleased if you'd pour me another."

Then, suddenly, he doubled up in alarm,
A look of great fear on his face.
And gulping for air, he said, *"Give me a bone,*
Or I might just end up in disgrace."

"I'm clean out of bones", said the landlord.
"I've had none delivered today.
I'll see if I've got some in t' freezer."
And with that, walked slowly away.

So! Arnold stood there, nearly crying,
'Cos he knew he'd been took for a ride.
His teeth wer' gripped tight on t' door handle.
And he knew he daren't set foot outside.

Then! He got to the point of explosion.
And suddenly Arnold turned white.
And stiff legged he walked to the front door,
And bid everybody, *"Goodnight."*

THE BEANO SONG

Every Thursday morning, it drops behind the door.
Little Jimmy jumps out of bed,
It's just the thing he's waited for,
He hurries to collect it,
Starts reading right away.
Can't even eat his breakfast
'Cos today's his favourite day.

Chorus
And it's read by lads,
And it's read by their dads,
It's a national institution.
This comic's a cut above the rest,
The Beano simply is the best,
It's loved by generations,
From toddlers to old men.
Victoria would have been amused
If it had been round then.

Now, the monks were vowed to silence,
Not a man could make a sound,
Then through the snow a paper boy
Came trudging on his round.
He accidently put a Beano
Through the cloister door.
Now the monks get Beano every week
And laugh until they roar.

Chorus

Now rich great grandad Jonah Smith
Was dying in his bed.
His greedy relatives rubbed their hands
"*It won't be long*", they said.
Then great grandson put a Beano
In the old man's hand.
The old lad sat up chuckling loud
And shouted, "*I feel grand.*"

Chorus

If depression comes to you
Or if you're feeling sad, Go out and buy a Beano,
Soon you'll be feeling glad.
It's far better than a tonic,
It's got everything we're after.
We think the Beano should receive
The Queen's award for laughter.

Chorus

Old man crossing road   Chimney Sweep
Eye sight not so good   Climbing stack
Along comes a motor car   He fell down
Old man in box of wood   And broke his back.

(Rejected by *The Beano*, 1952)

If the butter runs,
Can the tomato ketchup.

(Accepted by *The Beano*, 1952)

THE REUNION

I had a drink, one afternoon,
Not so long ago,
And met up with a pal of mine,
That I used to know.

We talked about the good old days
That now are long gone by
Over pints of beer we ordered
In our turn, did him and I.

At three o' clock, we heard a call,
"Last orders!" was the shout,
And so we got another one,
Before they threw us out.

"I know a club quite near," said he,
"That opens up at three."
So in we went and got another round
Did him and me.

Round of drinks on round of drinks,
"It isn't your round, it's mine."
"Put your money away and let me pay."
"Hell fire, it's half past nine."

How many we had I couldn't say,
We must have had a load,
We had one more for old time's sake,
Then several for the road.

It was midnight when we parted,
And I staggered down the street.
I might have had a skinful,
But I fancied somethin' t' eat.

Although I'd had no dinner,
Although I'd had no tea,
I knew my wife at home,
Would have a meal just made for me.

I tiptoed up the garden path
And opened up the door.
I stumbled in and through my fog
I heard the missus roar.

She bellowed down from up the stairs,
These words cut through my fog,
*"Your dinner, tea and supper's
keeping warm - inside the dog!"*

This poem has been sponsored by a very fat
but grateful dog.

How I Stopped Smoking

I 'adn't 'ad a cigarette for two an' 'alf days,
As I drifted in a lifeboat on rough seas.
I'd even tried to smoke a bit of torn pants leg,
But it gave me such a cough and made me wheeze.

When at last I made the shore on a small desert isle,
I found that smoking seaweed made me ill.
And I swore that when at last I got to civil-is-ation,
Of proper cigarettes I'd smoke my fill.

When rescue came at last just a few days later on,
I'd chewed my fingernails down to the bone,
But the boat that came to save me not one man aboard it smok
And by then I would have smoked a soggy prawn.

When they dropped me on the shore I jumped aboard a bus,
Even though I didn't know where it was bound.
I dropped to my hands and knees searching underneath the seats,
But not the tiniest of fag ends could be found.

So I went and sat next to the only passenger on board,
And I told him of my shipwreck and my plight,
When he reached into his pocket and withdrew a pack of fags,
The whole world seemed to suddenly turn bright.

I took one in my shaking hands and put it to my trembling lips,
It was then that fate decided to be cruel,
After click, click, click, click, click, click, click,
He said, *"I'm sorry but my lighter's out of fuel."*

RUDOLPH

In Russia, some years back,
In Communist days,
Lived Rudolph Oleg, a man set in his ways.
An out and out Communist, an intransigent Red,
"The Kremlin's best servant", his wife always said.

One day the Olegs discussed upon whether
Rain, snow or sleet would be the day's weather.
Mrs. Oleg said, *"Today will be snow."*
But shaking his head, hard, Rudolph cried, *"No,*
I look at those clouds and I see very plain,
That today, in Moscow, we'll only have rain."

Just at that moment a deluge came down,
Wetting the roofs and the streets of the town.
His wife said, *"Oh, Rudolph, you clever old Red."*
"Ah! Rudolph the Red knows rain, dear," he said.

GONE BUT NOT FORGOTTEN

(T' Concert in t' Sky)

I'll tell thee a tale to amaze thi.
Id'll mek thi sit up i' thi cheer,
Could gi' thi a laff or a chuckle,
Or id might mek thi skrike i' thi beer.

If tha ed aw t' money i' England,
There's summat thi brass couldn'd buy;
Memories o' bygone Lancyshire fooak,
As Ah think o' yon concert i' t' sky.

Frank Randle wor standin' at microphooan,
He wur drunk - 'e'd bin suppin aw day.
*"Aw supped some ale toneet - baay
Led's get on wi t' do reyt away."*

"I'ds a Lancashire free n' easy neet."
His drunken eeen moved around t' cast
Of bygone Lancashire talent,
Aw present, bud every one passed.

"Reyt Gracie, thee start," said Randle an' burped.
An Gracie stood up, clogs n' shaw,
Hoo sang *'Sally'*, and *'th'* owd *Aspidistra'*
An' ended wi *'Sing As Wi Go'*.

Jimmy Clitheroe played his accordian,
Him and Ted Ray drove 'em wild.
Sam Laycock then towd 'em some dialect,
T' same as way do up at t' Fylde.*

"An' neaw fer a treat," slurred Randle,
*"Duettists, the best thad way've ad.
An act as defies definition -
George Formby performs wi 'is dad."*

Thi went through aw young George's favrites,
Cleyned winders wi owd Mr. Woo,
Leyned on t' lamp wi Aunt Maggie,
An sang o' some Blackpoo' rock too.

Th' applause as thi finished wur deeafnin,
Wi' th' audience merrier and merrier.
"An neaw for a change," sheawted Randle,
"Ladies and Gentlemen - Kathleen Ferrier."

18

Kathleen sung just like a linnet,
'*Th' 'oly City*' - '*Crimond*' - '*Bless this heawse*'.
Tears flooad - aye even fro' Randle,
All t' place wur as quiet as a meawse.

I' mi minds eye Ah looked aw reawnd t' room,
Nowt bud a seet fer sore een.
Ah cudn'd 'elp skrikin' an' thinkin'
Hoo wur t' finest thad ever there's been.

"*Ah believe t' suppers ready,*" grinned Randle,
An brushed down his owd chequered suit.
"*Black peys - it's a musical evenin' - so
Wur aw 'evin' musical fruit.*"

Albert Modley wur skennin' through t' winder.
He'd bin watchin' t' performers on t' mike.
"*Tha nod cummin' in,*" shouted Randle,
"*Id's Lanky - tha're on'y a Tyke.*"

Reg Dixon then geet up on th' organ,
Playin' fer all 'e wor worth.
Ah slowly cum deawn to reality,
Me and mi thowts back t' earth.

So if thad aw t' money in England,
There's summat thi brass couldn't buy.
If tha lived fro neaw till Domesday:
A ticket fer t' concert i' t' sky.

Several poems and monologues in this book were
written for the Fylde Folk Festival Poetry
Competition. The line, "*Sam Laycock then towd 'em
some dialect, T' same as way do, up at t' Fylde*"
refers to this competition.

A Victorian Melodrama

On a cold, blustery, wintery night,
The drunkard emerged from the pub.
He reeled and staggered his way down the street,
As though he'd drunk his ale by the tub.

Back home in her cold, lonely attic
His daughter awaited in fear
For the noisy return of her father.
The drunkard - a slave to the beer.

Tonight it would be just as usual.
Exactly the same as before.
He'd find some small fault with her cleaning -
Thrash her with his belt to the floor.

She longed for the old days with mother.
When father was upright and true.
A well-known and highly respected
Campaigner against *'Devil's Brew'*.

It started one day in November,
When mother had suffered and died.
He wept with a grief that was hurtful,
But couldn't control it inside.

Some well-meaning friends - to console him,
Gave comfort from out of a glass.
This lead to his road of destruction
Along which all drunkards must pass.

That small glass then lead to another
Which made his grief slowly subside,
Until he could not do without it,
The *'Devil's Brew'* then was his bride.

The noise of the gate flying open,
The slur of his feet on the path
Brought her back to realisation.
She waited to confront his wrath.

The firegrate has not been blackleaded,
His slippers were not by the door.
He gave her a stinging backhander;
She fell - with a thud - to the floor.

Her right hand grabbed hold of the poker;
She crashed it down hard on his head;
A realisation came on her;
Her father, the drunkard, was dead!

Outside, all the gas lights burned dimly;
She walked in the cold midnight air;
The arm of the law on her shoulder,
Her face showing utter despair.

Thrown in a damp lonely dungeon,
A straw-covered floor for her bed.
The judge gave his verdict of *'Guilty'*.
She'd hang by the neck until dead.

This story is true - that I swear it.
It happened a century ago.
She was my grandmother's mother,
That's my family's sad tale of woe.

LANCASHIRE PRIDE

Reflectin' o' Lancashire - Present and Past,
And Lancashire products, built solid to last.
Weer t' quality an' t' craftsmen stond firm, side bi side,
Wod's med 'ere i' Lancashire's med 'ere wi' pride.

Generations agoo id wer weyvin' an' t' loom.
Aye, t' best i' aw t' world an' id browt us a boom.
When t' sheds wer demolished, Ah stood theer an' cried,
Fer t' memory o' t' weyvers thad weyved theer, wi pride.

Way've pride i' eawr ceawnty, an' pride in eawr rose,
An' pride in eawr people an' eawses thad shows.
Poor quality, Lancastrians 'll ne'er abide,
Fer nowt licks eawr quality; nowt beats eawr pride.

Mention Lancashire products thro'eawt t' British Isles,
An' fra Devon to Lanark they'll sey wi' a smile
Thad Lancashire goods 'r aw tested an' tried.
If Lancashire med it, thi med id wi' pride.

Ah've sed aw mi life, an' 'll sey till Ah dee,
An' aw yo' abeawt 'ere are beaynt t' agree,
Thad wen choosin' a product, like choosin' a bride,
Choose Lancashire made, tha'll ged Lancashire pride.

Way've tekken sum knocks, an' bin t' brunt o' sum jokes.
Fooak think wer aw clogs, fact'ry chimneys an' smoke.
But aw t' other ceawnties faw deawn bi t' wayside,
They've ony geet quality - way've quality AND pride.

Eawr Lancashire fooak an' eawr Lancashire teawns,
Eawr fact'ries an' mills, aw eawr ups an' eawr deawns,
But thro' thick n' thin way'll never let slide
Thad one thing that med us, eawr LANCASHIRE PRIDE.

FRED'S NEW WIG

Fred Smith is a vain sort of fellow,
Who's been bald the best part of his life.
He got himself one of them toupees,
Well, he bought it, he said, *"to please t' wife"*.

It looked a reyt mess when he wore it,
Just like a flat cap on 'is head.
It looked every bit worth a shilling.
Like something th' apprentice 'as med.

It's perched on his head like a tomcat.
Might as well have t' price tag hanging down.
It's split up one side (for a partin') an it's ginger,
But the bit of hair he has is brown.

I remember t' first time that he wore it,
He walked into t' club wi' a grin.
Owd 'Arry, the stupid door keeper
Give him t' book and said, *"'ere lad, sign in"*.

Fred looked, he were quite flabber-gasted.
He said, *"Don't you know who it is?"*
*"I don't care if tha t' Queen Lizzie's 'usband,
Tha stays out there until tha signs this"*.

So with that, Fred whipped off his headgear,
Turned it round back to front bout ado.
*"Oh! Why didn't you say. It looks much better that way,
But it still makes thee look a reyt foo'"*.

Now, Tommy the barman he's ignorant
And I knew he'd have something to say.
He said, *"Lads 'll give thee a reyt wiggin'"*
And, *"There's no strap for beer, you've toupee"*.

And with that he guffawed with laughter,
He rocked and he bellowed and roared,

He laughed 'til he cried, then clutching his side,
He sunk, laughing still, to the floor.

By now Fred was getting deflated,
And gave Tommy a very hard stare.
But Tommy had partly recovered and said,
"You'll look better with a bit of fresh 'air".

At one point I went into t' toilets,
Fred were there havin' a pee.
And somebody said, *"I don't know about hare,
It looks more like a rabbit to me"*.

Fred stood this all night without flinching,
As slowly his beer he did quaff.
'Til a silly old short-sighted barman,
told him, *"Peak of your cap's fallen off"*.

He rushed out o' t' club nearly cryin',
And I really felt sorry for Fred,
When a bloke at the door said, *"Don't it make your scalp sore,
When you wear Shredded Wheat on your head?"*

The moral of this tale is simple,
If you haven't much hair on your head,
Don't spend all your brass on a toupee,
Or you might finish up like poor Fred.
For there's nowt to be ashamed of in baldness,
It comes as a natural thing.
But if you insist on a toupee,
Knit one yourself out of string.

❧❧

TRIBUTE TO AMERICA

There's a place 'cross th' Atlantic as breeds folk wi' big gobs,
A place full o' folk wi' loose slates.
An' on top o' big gobs, they have big daft ideas
Like they get in the United States.

Don't show them a thing you're impressed with,
They'll tell you they've seen it before.
If it's big they'll tell you they've bigger,
If it's something you've got, they've got more.

Like

*"See that chimney over there, it stands three hundred feet.
My grandad built it with his mate in three week - what a feat!"*

*"Waaay that's nuthin'.
My grandpaw built a chimney
Half as tall again
And built it in a week n' half
Just him and two more men."*

*"See that ship that's docking, they named it after t' Queen,
My brother helped to build it, the finest ship I've seen."*

*"Waaay that's nuthin'.
Back home in New York City
When children finish school
They've bigger boats in Central Park
They're sailing in the pool."*

*"See that building over there, built sixty years ago,
It holds a thousand people - the biggest one I know."*

*"Waaay that's nuthin'.
We've buildings twenty times as big
That hold a million folk
And built a hundred years ago -
Makes yours look a joke."*

"Aye, I'm not surprised," said the Englishman,
*"That your lot have to pile 'em,
Inside your building twice as big -
IT'S A LUNATIC ASYLUM."*

DONALDO'S TIN

MUTINY ON THE *BOUNTY*

A boat set sail for Tahiti,
'*Bounty*' wer' what it were called,
And Bligh wer' the name of its skipper,
Christian wer' t' mate so I'm told.

Neaw th' Admiralty sent Bligh to th' island,
(wi t' price of bread getting so steep)
'Cos if they could bring back a plant as were grown there,
They could feed all t' slave labour on t' cheap.

But instead of going t' route that were normal,
Route were they'd keep warm and dry.
They went round Cape Horn and got soaked for a month,
And they near froze to death except Bligh.

Sailing at last in calm water
A sailor cried in his tot,
"*I've getten no cheese on mi dinner*
'Cos captain's swiped all t' bloody lot."

Now Bligh were a man of good hearin',
An' he heard this through t' thin wooden wall,
So for callin' the captain a robber,
Had him whipped as a lesson to all.

At last, they set foot in Tahiti,
But t' natives wi' t' men wouldn't dine,
'Cos it weren't the done thing - but if you fancied his wife
You could take her to bed any time.

They got the plants growin' in boxes,
Loaded them all on board t' boat,
But sailors couldn't wash any soxes
Or sup water to quench a parched throat.

'Cos temperature down under t' deck head,
'Ad risen o'er a 'undred an' three,
'An if t' plants didn't get all the water they wanted,
They'd wilt down over t' boxes an' dee.

One sailor got real thirsty,
An' bad water from t' bilges he supped,
Which sent him off his head an' he went up to Bligh
An' called him a swine; reyt abrupt.

Christian knew just what had happened.
He took ladle from out t' water cask.
But Bligh punced it out of his hand an' he said,
"*If tha're wantin' some water tha'll ask.*"

Fletcher wer reyt disappointed,
He turned round and bashed Bligh in t' gob,
"*Tha's gone too far, I'm tekin' thi boat*
and givin' misel' captain's job."

Bligh thought that Christian was joking.
He said, *"Lad, you 'aven't a hope,*
When th' Admiralty find out about it,
You'll dangle on th' end of a rope."

They put Bligh and his cronies in t' longboat
Wi' food and provisions enough.
They shouted, *"Tarra mi owd flower."*
Bligh just replied, *"B*****r off."*

Bligh paddled around for a fortnight or more,
Till his feet on dry land he did set.
He wished he could fly back to England,
But planes weren't invented just yet.

At long last, he got back to Blighty,
And legged it to London real quick,
To tell t' Lord o' th' Admiralty about it,
An' he didn't half gi' Christian some stick.

They gave him a boat and some sailors,
A boat wi' masts mighty and tall.
They wer going to give him a submarine,
But they weren't invented and all.

He searched round the world's seven oceans
To find Christian and pay him his dues,
But though he saw nothing of Christian,
He saw Hindus, Moslems and Jews.

What happened to Christian's a mystery,
With stories uncertain and vague.
Some say he came back to England,
And some say he died of the plague.

But Fletcher were smitten wi' conscience
For lobbin' 'is mate into t' lake.
He wanders all night on the foredeck,
Hence the term... *"Christians Awake!"*

THE CLOG FIGHTER

In a town just east of Blackburn,
Near the Church and Ossie border,
In Accrington, lived Cloggie Joe,
A man of sheer disorder.

He were t' world clog-feytin champion,
An' knew all t' clog-feytin tricks,
From lashin' out with both his feet,
To sneaky, back-heel flicks.

He'd beat the best for miles around.
Held the '*Golden Clogs*' award.
He fought for t' Northwest Tripe Dressers,
And usually swept the board.

But Joe were a dirty feyter,
And he liked to set the pace.
He'd chew on lumps of garlic,
Which made him hard to face.

From breathed out clouds of acrid fumes,
Opponents fell away.
Advantage Joe, he'd come in low,
And punce 'em where they lay.

Now Joe got reyt conceited,
And he strutted down the street
In his new, lead-weighted training clogs
(To give him stronger feet).

He swaggered in t' *Duck and Trumpet*,
Where t' landlord Cross-eyed Mick
Stirs his beer wi' owd clog irons
- to give it stronger kick.

Joe's girlfriend were sat there, in t' corner,
St-stutterin' Bertha Magee.
She'd a figure like lamp-leeter's donkey,
And a face like a busted settee.

Joe got her a pint of lampoil shandy,
And needing something stronger to face her,
He ordered a pint o' best bitter,
And half a pint Iron Brew chaser.

He were taking t' drinks over to Bertha,
When a stranger came clattering in,
Wearing the biggest pit boots
That Joe, or his cronies, had sin.

A gasp came from old 'Arry Pickersgill,
Like a rapid-deflating car tyre,
'Cos he knew who it were, and he knew why he'd come,
And he knew then that t' fat were in t' fire.

He looked at Joe's clogs wi' a smirk on his face,
Looked Joe up an' down wi' a sneer.
You could hear a pin drop when he said wi' a growl,
"*Tha fancies thisel' so I hear.*"

Up from his seat jumped old 'Arry,
And spoke up so all t' pub could hear,
"*It's Pit Boot Punce Champion fray Wigan,
An' he won t' Lonsdale Boot just last year.*"

"*You're challenging me?*" said Joe wi' a laugh.
"*I've come for thi crown,*" said the lad,
And Cross-eyed Mick said, "*If tha're challenging Joe
Tha's got to be barmy, or mad.*"

They 'kicked off' outside t' *Duck and Trumpet*,
Puncin' each other around
From one side o' t' town to the other,
But neither o' t' feyters went down.

They fought until long after sunset,
Till both were exhausted and raw,
And as both knew that none could lick t' other,
The feyters agreed on a draw.

Later, back in t' *Duck and Trumpet*.
They both were the toast of the town,
And they stood with their arms round each other,
As pint after pint, they put down.

They were so full of bloated importance
As they spoke of each others careers.
Neither heard Daisy's, *"Excuse me."*
Her request to pass fell on deaf ears.

"Excuse me," she said a bit louder,
"Will you let me get through to the bar?"
But Bob and Joe had decided
That they weren't going to move very far.

They say she moved faster than lightnin'
As she hitched up her skirt to her knees,
And a Double-legged-round-house-back-slider,
Felled both Bob and Joe like two trees.

She stepped over both fallen heroes,
And ordered a drink at long last,
And said without batting an eyelid,
"Tha should get out o' t' way when you're asked."

What happened to 'em after's a mystery,
'Cos neither was heard of again.
Some say they both emigrated,
And some say that they both died of shame.

The moral is, if you're a fighter,
With fist or with boot or with clog.
It isn't the size of the dog in the fight,
It's the size of the fight in the dog.

DUGDALE'S DAY TRIP TO THE SEA

In 'istry there's been many 'eroes,
Who've stood firm when t' goin' got rough,
And won out against all opposition.
Such men are made of strong stuff.

The one thing that in 1940,
Kept us, in Great Britain, free
From 'itler; weren't Winston's great planning;
It were Dugdale's day trip to the sea.

More stirring than George and the Dragon.
More moving than Senna-Pod Tay.
A story of 'eroe's and villains
Is what I shall tell thi today.

Dugdale were makin' his way to the beach,
An hopin' the weather were grand,
He'd a brown paper bag full of butties,
'Cos he fancied a picnic on t' sand.

When he got to the beach it were crowded
Wi' folk, in boats, puttin' to sea,
"*I'm goin' to Dunkirk for the day,*" said a bloke,
"*If you'll help wi' th' oars I'll tek thee.*"

Dugdale got seated in t' vessel
And he didn't know whether to laugh
When he saw that the 'boat' he were sat in,
Wer' only a little tin bath.

"*We're goin,*" said Dugdale's new bathmate,
"*'Cos our lads over there have got beat,*"
"*I don't follow football,*" said Dugdale,
"*We only played tig in our street.*"

That both had no qualifications,
In bathmanship soon became clear,
When it took 'em four hours and a quarter,
To get to the end of the pier.

On top of their poor navigation,
Their joe-egg-raphy knowledge was slight,
And they thought that Dunkirk was turn right at the lighthouse,
And just above Ramsgate, on t' right.

It took 'em all mornin' to get there,
Dugdale were tired as could be,
An' his bag full of butties were soggy an' damp,
'Cos they'd fallen three times in the sea.

They pulled the bath up on to t' shingle,
And some fellows in uniform cheered
And ran down the beach and kissed Dugdale.
(Which was something that he'd always feared.)

They started the naval bombardment,
Dugdale were shook, it were plain.
He thowt it were thunder, and turned up his collar,
And said, "*Nay, I 'ope it don't rain.*"

So he thought he'd best take a quick paddle,
Wi' t' pants legs rolled up, and t' knees bare.
Now, - THAT, - was the move that saved Britain,
'Cos his butties were left lyin' there.

Onto the beach strutted five or six men,
All weighed down wi' medals galore.
And one, wi' a 'tash like a brocken-off toothbrush,
Goose-stepped out front, on the shore.

'itler spotted the bag full of butties,
And finding them filled with boiled ham,
Gave one to each of his of his henchmen.
And said, "*Zis makes quite a change from plum jam.*"

He were skimmin' some pebbles on t' water,
An' bouncin' em over his bath,
When he saw that they'd pinched all his butties.
Dugdale gave vent to some wrath.

He jumped up and down in the water.
And checkin' his braces were tight,
Up over t' beach to this geyser wi' t' 'tash,
He sped in a mad headlong flight.

When he got there, they'd finished his butties,
And he stared at his bag full of crumbs,
Then he up and he hit 'em all 'ard in the teeth,
- And he hit one wi' no teeth in the gums.

His fists were a blur on the vision
As he gave each offender a clout,
And three seconds after he'd started
He'd laid all the six of 'em out.

They lay on the beach bruised and sulkin'
Their faces all hurtin' an' sore,
An' he told 'em, if he ever saw them again
He'd set to and he'd give 'em some more.

Back at the bath, right dejected,
'Cos he'd had such a terrible day,
He seated three extra passengers down
And rowed very s-l-o-w-l-y away.

Later at the edge of the water,
Adolph stared out in despair,
Gazing at t' white cliffs o' Dover,
And knowing that Dugdale were there.

So he turned and he said to his cronies,
"*Though all Britain's armies have fled,
If we go, we may come across Dugdale,
Let's attack bloody Russia instead.*"

Now you are in on the story,
Of why 'itler spared you and me.
In those dark days of June 1940.
It wer' Dugdale's day trip to the sea.

75 Pence

Mr. and Mrs. Ramsbottom
Are feeling reyt proud of their lad
He's set 'imself up in a business
The finest job Albert has had.

He'd tried lots of different vocations,
Wherever he worked, he'd not stop;
He completed a correspondence course
And opened a swank barber's shop.

He couldn't get hold of a barber's pole
Covered in stripes white and red,
So he painted his stick with the horse's-head
handle and put that up outside instead.

He weren't very good when he started,
'is haircutting made people laugh.
He went through twelve combs the first hour
He kept cutting the darn things in half.

He cut holes in customers' collars
And one or two holes in the chair,
He even cut holes in the carpet
But claimed that wer' *"fair wear and tear"*.

One day he wer' sharpening his scissors
On t' doorstep, just outside t' shop,
When a customer trod on his fingers;
And it hurt, and made Albert stop.

"'aircut, quick about it,"
He said in a voice Albert knew,
It wer Bully Boy Badger,
who every playtime had clouted young Albert at schoo'

Though Albert had recognised Badger,
The opposite did not occur.
So he started to hack with his scissors,
Making a mess of his hair.

He cut some big chunks from the top of his head
And cut some great steps at the side,
He thought it the finest of haircuts
And his chest fairly puffed up with pride.

He was hacking at Badger's left sideboard
And wishing his fingers weren't sore,
When he slipped; and cut the lad's ear off,
And it fell with a thud to the floor.

Albert hoped Badger hadn't noticed,
So he did some neat footwork right there,
Pushed the ear through a crack in the floorboard,
Where it fell on a pile of old hair.

He then quickly finished his snipping
And Bully Boy reached for his hat,
Albert stood there nearly crying
As Badger said *"'Ow much is that?"*

"*75 pence*", replied Albert;
He'd have charged a bit less were he wise,
For Bully Boy guessed what had happened,
when his hat fell down over his eyes.

"*Gi' me mi ear back*", said Badger,
Albert said, "*75 pence.*"
And he started to brush Badger's coat down,
To show that he meant no offence.

"*No ear, no money*", yelled Badger,
"*No money, no ear*", Albert cried
When into the shop walked Sam Ogglethwaite.
So both asked if Sam would decide.

"*This mon won't gi' mi me ear back*,"–
"*75 pence he owes me,
I can't run a business for nothing,
I never do haircuts for free.*"

They both gave their versions to Sammy,
The atmosphere grew very tense,
"*Gi' mi me ear back*", said Badger.
Albert said, "*75 pence.*"

Then Sam said "*I've got a suggestion,
If Badger gives t' money to me,
And Albert brings Badger's left ear back,
Things would work out twixt us three.*"

Badger liked Sammy's idea,
And said that it made lots of sense,
"*And if Albert will give me a discount for damage.*"
Albert said, "*75 pence.*"

Then Albert said, "*Sam, you're a joiner,
Will you take up the floorboards for me?*"
"*Aye, I'll do it a fortneet on Wednesday,
that's the earliest date that I've free.*"

Badger gave Sammy the money,
And stormed out as mad as could be,
And when Albert knew he wouldn't hear him,
Shouted, "*Who wants yer seventy-five p?*"

Now that the business was settled,
Albert asked why Sam were here,
And wondered why on Sam's calm countenance
Appeared a sharp look of great fear.

"*I did come in for a haircut,
but seeing the mess, that tha's med,
I'll go to the butcher on t' corner,
And see if he'll chop it instead.*"

THE BALLAD OF SERGEANT DOBSON

I'll tell you a terrible story
Of some policeman's unfortunate plight
'Cus robbers have got really cheeky
And pinched summat vital one night

Police Sergeant Dobson decided
He'd best take a walk out the back.
When he got to the gentlemen's toilet
What he saw stopped him dead in this track.

'Cus thieves had bin there the last evening,
Bob looked for the toilet in vain
But the lousy, light-fingered intruders
Had pinched toilet, bowl, cistern and chain

He walked through the door to the closet
And nearly fell down a big hole:
Instead of the '*porcelain pony*',
Just the ball-cock stuck out from the wall.

He's sat with his legs crossed all weekend
Signing summonses, statements and so on
What's worse there's no chance of an early arrest
And the police have got nothing to go on.

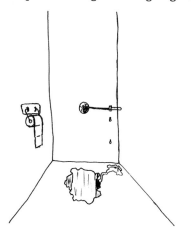

NICKED NICK

The Town Hall clock struck ten to two
One dark December neet
A lonely policeman traipsed up brew
Upon his frozen beat

His hands were dead inside his gloves
His ears and nose were blue
His feet were froze inside his shoes
His assets frozen too

A noise from off a nearby roof
Made frozen Policeman stop
In time to see a man emerge
From out a chimbley top

It made him feel elated
His thoughts began to soar
He'd been a policeman 20 years,
Never caught a thief before

So he scammered up a drainpipe
And then without a pause
He shouted, "*You're arrested,
Dressed up like Santa Claus.*"

The burglar is upset at this,
"*You can't nick me*", he sings,
"*I'm really Father Christmas,
And I'm giving all these things!*"

The Policeman laughed until he cried,
"*Oh yes I can and worse,
I'm charging you with trespassing
And burglary in reverse.*"

T' DANCIN' DUCK

I'll tell thi a tale that's as true as can be
It's as true as I'm pushin' this truck.
Concerning a villain called Gradwell
And 'is antics one night wi' a duck

Gradwell came into my local one night
Wi' a duck and tin box on his arm
An' he told us the following story
He said, "*This duck 'asn't come from a farm.*"

"*Observe now this talented creature
His name is Donaldo the Great,
And his foot-tapping, heel-clicking capers
Make Fred Astaire look second rate.*"

He then put the tin on the counter
And placing Donaldo on top
Said, "*Just watch him dance like a trooper.*"
Donaldo then started to hop.

He lifted one foot then the other
Then he clattered away on the tin
And people came into the pub from afar
To find out the cause of the din.

The landlord, a tightfisted bugger,
Saw this would make people flock in
So he made Mr Gradwell an offer
Ten pounds for the duck and the tin.

"*Ten pounds for this duck! Think I'm quackers?
It could make thi a fortune some day.
If you really are wanting this creature
Fifty is what you must pay.*"

A bargain was struck with a handshake
And Gradwell, a smirk on his face
Put the brass into his pocket
And hurried away from the place

Donaldo meanwhile was still making
A cacophonous row on his tin
In top hat, duck tails and a dickie
And a bow-tie stuck under his chin.

Far into the night he kept dancing
And no-one could sleep for the din
Of Donaldo's web-footed terpsichory
As he clattered away on his tin.

At long last there came a policeman
Whose knowledge of con tricks was wide
He lifted the duck and the lid of the tin
And blew out the candle inside.

T' SEAWND O' T' SEA

(A conversation between father and son)

"What's yon seawnd, Ah'm 'earin' fayther?"
"That, lad's t' seawnd o' t' sea."
"An is id blue as tha towd mi, fayther?"
"Aye; blue, lad, as con be."
"An are white 'orses ridin' t' spray
Weer t' waves are breykin all o'er t' bay.
O' t' gowden sond weer t' childer play?"
"Oh lad; if tha could but see."

"Mi mam said id'd seawnd like this."
"That's reyt - so hoo said."
"When hoo gi mi 'er goodneet kiss
An' tucked mi up I' bed.
When th' angels geet 'er off up yon
Ah couldn'd see weer hoo'd gone.
Wi bein' blind - mi lamps were dun"
"Aye, God rest her, lad."

"Ah wish mi mam wur 'ere neaw dad."
"Aye lad Ah con tell."
"Does it mek thi feel reyt sad?"
"Aye lad, Ah could yell."
"Bud we'll enjoy this sea and sond.
Will t' tek me near an' owd mi hond?
Fayther, yon sea seawnds really grand."
"Aye id seawnds reyt well."

"Conta hear yon breykers roarin?"
"Aye lad, thad Ah con."
"Are there gulls oe'r t'watter sooarin'?"
"Aye - 'underds on 'em son."
"Con we goo an paddle in t' foam
Just thee and me, Dad, on eawr own
An' listen t' sea till t' time t' go whooam"
"Aye lad, let's hev fun."

"Did mi mam like t' seawnd o' t' sea?"
"Aye lad, thad hoo did."
"When did hoo last come 'ere wi thee?"
"When tha wer just a brid."
"An' neaw mi mam can't come no mooer
Fer neaw hoo's gone through Heaven's dooer."
"Aye lad - Heaven forbid."

"Wod's yon seawnd Ah'm 'earin'fayther? –
Whatever con it be?
Id seawnds just like tha cryin' fayther?" –
"Neah lad; id's just seawnd o' t' sea."

34

BOLLINGTON

I chanced upon a wayside pub
In Bollington one day
While stopping for a pint or two
To help me on my way

Outside *The Queen's* the Morris men
And Morris ladies too
Danced around fantastically
And drank their foaming brew

Now Morris folk all like a good beer.
Will only drink the best,
So as I looked and saw the sign
I knew I'd reached my quest

Robinson's Beer proclaimed the sign.
I ordered at the bar
And quaffed the golden nectar down
From out the foaming jar.

Mine hosts and staff were jovial,
The music and songs made my day,
It's *The Queen's* and *Robinsons* for me
Next time I'm Bollington way.

BOLLINGTON, Cheshire, Urb. Dist. 10m. S.W. of Manchester.
Industries inc. fine cotton spinning, rayon, nylon & silk spinning
& doubling, calico printing, paper staining & fabric dyeing.
E.C. Wed. Fam. 1,802. Pop. 5,313.

IN PRAISE OF SCHOOL MEALS

"Don't make me eat my dinner, Dinner Lady.
Don't make me eat this rubbish school grub.
If you make me force it down, I'll be sick all over town
Like my dad does on his way home from the pub."

"Don't make me eat my soup, please Dinner Lady
Don't make me eat this leek and beetroot broth
There's a letter from my mum which says food's bad for my tum
And besides it smells like pigswill from a trough."

Chorus

You frighten us to death, dear Dinner Lady,
You fill us with an awful sense of doom
You have us in your power, every day, just for an hour
As you goose step up and down the dining room.

"Don't make me eat my fish, please, Dinner Lady,
Don't make me eat this luke warm piece of skate.
It fills me full of dread and I'm sure the thing's not dead,
'Cos it's flopping up and down upon my plate."

"I hate stale sloppy cabbage, Dinner Lady,
I've an allergy to Brussel sprouts and beans
If you make me eat my fill, then I really will be ill
And my pink face won't be pink it will be green."

Chorus

"My Spotted Dick's got bits in, Dinner Lady,
And you know that lumpy custard makes me queasy
If you make me eat my pud' I'll be sick all of a sud'
I'll show you if you like, it's really easy."

"Please may we leave the table, Dinner Lady,
Our plates are empty, please don't make us stay
What you think is in our bellies, we have spooned into our wellies
Which we'll empty down the toilet, then we'll play."

Chorus

35

No Time Fer Skrikin

In an Accrington pub, 'angs a picthur,
In a frame, on a wall, o'er a bar.
It's geet one mon's name, Tommy Atkins,
An' a date, July fost in t' Gret War.

"Give us a gill, Eli, tha'art quiet toneet."
Eli tarned an' stared Tommy in th' een.
"Joe Entwistle's mam's geet a telegram."
"BloodyWar! T' lad wer only nineteen."

"Wod the hell meks 'em tek yon King's shillin'
An rush to fire t' musket an' t' baw.
Who the 'ell gives a damn wod'll 'appen
What do they care, aye nowt ad aw."

"It's allreyt fer yon mon on t' pooasters
as tha skens at, pinned up all o'er t' place,
finger stuck eawt,- Country, neeads thi,
Th' all thing's a blasted disgrace!"

Owd Bert, tapped 'is pipe eawt on t' fender.
And slowly took th' eyd fro' 'is gill.
"But fer our lads ower theer, Tom,
Tha'd answer to owd Kaiser Bill."

Tommy thowt 'ard as he thraipsed ooam, up t' lone,
Heaw wer 'e beawn tell t' wife
He'd med a decision to goo an' enlist,
Aye even to lay deawn 'is life.

Jem Clegg barnin' t' lice fro' 'is gret cooat,
Stared eawt at t' claggy slutch o'er t' Somme
"Penny fer t' thowts Jem," axed Walter.
"Ah wish ah wer' boozin' back ooam."

"Yon Thwaitses an' Massey's an' Nuttall's best mild,
Ay mon, Ah con see Eli poo id,
Wi' th' 'eyd slarrin' deawn to t' bottom o' t' glass
An' no sign of owd Fritz's bullet."

"Tommy an' Bert 'll bi lobbin' 'em back,
an gooin' 'ooam plaistered on t' tram."
"Joe Entie warn'd bi gooin' na mooar,
Ah wonder if they've infoormed 'is Mam."

"Tha looks a gradely toff i' thi unifoorm Tom,
'Ev one wi' me fro' t' top shelf."
Eli gi' Tommy a handshake an' a tot.
"Good luck Tom, God bless an' good 'ealth."

Sarah Jane wer' creym stooanin' 'er dooer step,
Fer Tommy wer' soon hooam on leave.
He'd penned a few words fro' *'Somewhere in France'*
"Sithi soon bonny lass, durned thi grieve."

"Fix bayonets! Stand by! Three more minutes!"
Tommy stood to 'is ankles in t' nast.
Fire step. Ladders. Barbed wire an' grass sods,
Weer he lay, brocken-limbed fro yon blast.

Hoo looked at yon telegram, an' clutched owd o' t' kids.
Tears in 'er een gettin' wetter,
He'd set eawt aw wick fro t' station.
An' cum back in a government letter.

Suppin i' silence, snurchin back tears,
Owd Bert supped 'is gill, nowt wer' said,
Till Eli piped up, *"Dorned keep blamin' thi sel',*
Id isn't thy fault Tommy's dead."

In a Lancashire pub hongs a memr'y,
In a frame on a wa' o'er a bar,
Donated by Tommy's young widder,
An' a date, July fost, in t' Gret War.

Alan won the **Samuel Laycock Trophy** at the Fylde Folk
Festival, 1987, with this poem.

SPACE AGE VERSUS OLD AGE

When you and I are 82
What will there be for us to do?
The Nursing Homes will be 'choc-a-block',
There'll be no room for us, owd cock,
They'll catapult us into Space
To make way for a younger race
So there we'll be day after day
Just whizzing round the Milky Way

When you and I are 82 dear
There'll not be much to bring us cheer
I cannot walk - you've got the runs
And both of us have toothless gums
Our hair is white - our eyes are dim
Our legs and arms are pale and thin
Just one thing is saving our grace
We're out of sight up here in space!

When you and I are 82, love,
We'll view the planets from above
Peering at the earth from a space capsule
Feeling no end of a useless fool
The sun and moon our close relations
With absolutely no expectations
And is this what they've brought us to
Because we've got to 82?

For us no homemade meal or dish,
Nor yet a smell of chips and fish
They'll feed us tablets by the score
So they don't have to cook no more
And entertainment for old dears
Means harking back to yesteryears
To show them how they used to be
Young, fit and strong at 23!

But all that's gone for you and I
Just whizzing round and round the sky
And all that's left for you and me
Is dreams of days that used to be
Technology hasn't conquered age
It's imprisoned us within it's cage
So from my space chair, I'll gaze at you
That's all there's left for us to do!

A ROSE BY ANY OTHER NAME

Under t' Bull Brig i' Accrington,
T' River Hyndburn flooas,
Tha con allus tell as tha nearin'
Bi sniffin' an' foll'win' thi nooas,

Its reyt name is the Hyndburn,
Bud watter thad's clarty as ink,
Is known t' aw fooak i' Accy
Bi its nickname 'T' River Stink.'

It traycles its way under t' market,
Affoer reawlin' eawt just under t' brigs,
As black as a coyl miner's 'elmit,
An' a pong like a sty full o' pigs.

Ah used t' goo fishin' when Ah were a lad,
An smile ad aw t' memories id brings.
But salmon 'r treawt Ah didn't poo eawt,
But tin cans an' sum strange rubber things.

Wi used to play tig under t' culvert,
Tha 'ed ter wetch eawt if id rains.
Thad get a full blast o' th' efflant an' nast,
As teamed eawt i' torrents frae t' drains.

Aw t' gangs bilt bridges 'cross River Stink.
Wi bilt eawr's near t' Black Bull.
Bud froth an' slime med aw t' planks slippy
An way'd end up wi' wellingtons full.

If thad getten no wellies,
An wer messin' abeawt i' thi clogs,
Tha could walk across on aw t' bedsteads
An' prams, an' tin cans, an' deead dogs.

After way'd aw finished lakin',
We just wiped ussel on us clooas
An' walked up rooad eytin' threepennorth
O' chips thad wi bowt fro' Chip Joe's.

Bud neaw teawn planners er busy,
Brains 'av aw gone onto t' blink.
Thiv pooed deawn t' Black Bull an aw t' buildins
An' erected posh stoorers o'er t' Stink.

It's mebbe fert better thiv dun id
When Ah think of aw times theer in t' past,
Its a wonder wi didn' get typhoid,
Paddlin' in aw t' filth an' nast.

An when Ah think back on mi childhood,
Memry o' t' Stink really clings,
An' Ah think of aw t' times Ah went fishin',
Fer tin cans an' them strange rubber things.

B B & B B B B B F

Les Bond were stood in a pub one night,
When a stranger came rattlin' in.
He had an official collector's badge
And an official collecting tin.

"Good Evening, Sir", the man then said
*"My name is Arnold Lund,
and I'm collecting on behalf of the
Bolton, Burnley and Barrow in Furness
Boys' Brass Band Benevolent Fund."*

"You What?" He cried, and the man replied.

I said, *"My name is Lund,
and I'm collecting on behalf of the
Bolton, Burnley and Barrow in Furness
Boys' Brass Band Benevolent Fund!"*

"Eh?" He said, and the man went red.

I said, *"My name is Lund,
and I'm collecting on behalfof the
Bolton, Burnley and Barrow in Furness
Boys' Brass Band Benevolent Fund!"*

"You'll have to speak up, I can't hear you!"

"My name is Arnold Lund, and I'm collecting on behalf of the Bolton, Burnley and Barrow in Furness Boys' Brass Band Benevolent Fund!!!"

*"I'm sorry Mister Bolton I just cannot hear,
Will you tell me again the reason you're here."*

"Oh, bugger you!!!!", said Lund.
*"Aye, and bugger you and your
Bolton, Burnley and Barrow in Furness
Boy's Brass Band Benevolent Fund."*

A SHORTSIGHTED VIEW ON LIFE

It's more than just a rumour,
Life has a sense of humour
It makes us fall in bits as we grow old.
My teeth fell out, that's drastic,
So I wear some made of plastic
And my hair came out in handfulls so I'm bald.

Now my eyes are weak and weary
Everything is blurred and bleary
It's like peering, dimly, through a murky mist
People say "*Hello*", and talk as
I distort my face to focus
In a vain attempt to find out who it is.

So I hope that my myopia isn't catching.
I hope my eye myopia doesn't spread
'Cos you look a big disgrace
When you're screwing up your face
So I'll just have to get some glasses for my head.

I was cooking in the kitchen,
Cos my taste buds were just itchin'

For some culinary masterpiece, in haste
I was always good at makin'
A gooey chocolate cake in
A gooier chocolate sauce, with rum to taste
Isn't it strange that Rowntree's cocoa
Looks remarkably like Bisto
Well, anyone can make a blind mistake
But I really made a bugger
I mistook the salt for sugar
Would you like a slice of salty gravy cake?

So I hope that my myopia isn't catching
I hope my eye myopia doesn't spread
'Cos you look a big disgrace
When you're screwing up your face
So I'll just have to get some glasses for my head

I've been jogging, I've been training
To keep the weight from gaining
A sporting life's the only one for me
But I've had to give up cricket,
I can't see the ball or wicket
So I'm going to be a football referee
Then I visited an optician,
And I told him I was wishin'
For some spectacles to make my life complete
He agreed I'd trouble viewing
Then said, "*Sorry, nothin' doing,
I'm a butcher, I can only sell you meat.*"

So I hope that my myopia isn't catchin'
I hope my eye myopia doesn't spread.
'Cos you feel a big disgrace,
When you're screwing up your face
So I'll just have to get some glasses for my head,
I'll just have to get some spectacles instead.

I Wish I Could Pee Straight

I wish I could pee straight.
It's embarassing and sad
Peeing sideways at an angle.
I was like that as a lad.

Everyone laughs when I go to pee
and I stand sideways on to the wall.
It's always a field day for peepers and queers
When I go to obey Nature's call

Take Saturday last, just for instance
I were drunk, I'd been drinkin' all day,
An I took out my peg and peed all down the leg
Of a bloke who was stood yards away

His face turned bright purple wi' anger
As he shook all the pee from his shoe.
An' I ran, wi' my thingy still danglin'
As he shouted, *"You swine, was that you?"*

So I sent for an apparatus,
Which the manufacturers say
Will stop me from peeing round corners
And make me pee straight, straight away.

It arrived, complete with instructions.
It was then I began to have doubt
Cos mine is a left-handed donger
And they've sent me a right handed spout.

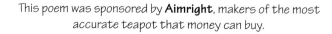

This poem was sponsored by **Aimright**, makers of the most
accurate teapot that money can buy.

IN MEMORY OF ALAN BOND (1940-92)
"A LANCASHIRE BALLADEER"

These next three poems were written by Alan's friends from the world of Lancashire folk-singing and dialect poetry; Mally Dow, Jim Atherton and Dave Dutton on learning from another friend, Bob Dobson, publisher of this book, about Alan's untimely death on 11th October 1992.

Another friend, poet Keith '*Scowy*' Scowcroft said the following few words at Alan's funeral - they describe him to a 'T'.

"…*Many are the folk-songs of hardship and tragedy. Perhaps they exist to prepare us for such as this (death), for life is as cruel and remorseless today as it has always been. Our happiness hangs by a single thread. Alan was well aware of this. He was, in the best sense of the word, a natural clown. He laughed his way through life and encouraged others to do the same, yet underneath that clown's exterior there lay a fine mind, a keen, observant eye and a wonderfully fertile imagination. All of which helped him to produce those poems we love so well … If he was on 'Mastermind', Alan's speciality would be 'People'. He was happiest in a crowd … I will always visualise him as 'The Lord of Misrule', holding court in a bar, 'bones' in one hand and a pint in the other, or issuing forth with a poem that would bring a tear to a glass eye … His family has lost a cornerstone; the folk world has lost an artist and an ambassador; Lancashire has lost a fine son; I have lost more than just a pal - much more like a brother, and the world has lost a friend - all much too soon.*"

In Memory of Alan Bond

Mally Dow (Thornton-Cleveleys)

I'm going to tell you a 'perfectly true story'
About a chap as most of you know.
He were known throughout England an 'Bondy',
And he left us a short while ago.

Now Bondy were known for his larkin'.
He enjoyed a good laugh and his ale,
He were famed for his stories and poems;
Aye! Bondy could tell a good tale.

He could have you in stitches in no time
And then, in t' next breath mek you cry.
I'd look round at all who were listening
And see not a single dry eye.

Folks would be holding their bellies wi' laughing
At the stories that Bondy did tell
About toupés and left-handed pee- spouts
And Dugdale and war time as well.

Now he told of a right special concert
To be held in yon place up in t' sky
With all t' Lancashire folk who'd passed over.
Now that one - it did make me cry.

Bondy pictured all t' folk there performing,
With Frank Randle, the drunken MC,
Gracie Fields were singing her heart out
And all of this concert were free.

It were free for t' folk already up there,
For us mortals - well, we couldn't go
No matter how much brass we might have,
We can't buy a ticket for that show.

Now then, God, in his infinite wisdom
Needed a new star for his 'Do'
And he looked down to see who were t' best here,
"Come on Bondy my lad, I want you."

So - he took him without even asking,
By gum we all had a good cry,
But you see Bondy were desperately needed
To star in yon concert in t' sky.

Now his words will be with us for ever,
Although he went with no time for goodbye.
And one day we'll all be together
For t' start of yon concert in t' sky.

Farewell to a 'Lanky' Balladeer

Jim Atherton (Darwen)

Them words I yerd fra Bob last neet
Fair med mi blood run cowd.
To think thad never mooar we'll meet,
Not like them days of owd.
For mi mind gooas back a two-thri year
To when wi stood theear side bi side.
We med 'em laugh, - some shed a tear
As wi stood theear side bi side.

44

Aye thee and me, wi said eawr piece
In far off Rochda' teawn,
And put th' Edwin Waugh lot at their ease,
Words said wi ne'er a freawn.
I watched tears well up like in thi een,
As tha read eawt 'Seawnd o' t' Sea'.
I were t' fost to shake thi hond lad,
When tha won yon 'Laycock' Cup.
And although I tried for id missell,
I were fain tha'd taen id up,
For tha'd tried an' tried for monny a year,
And coom near to t' winning pooast.
But tha won id though I com quite near,
And yet tha did na booast,
So neaw lad tha's bin cawed up yon,
Though monny years too soon.
Whil'st here tha were a gradely mon,
So they'll welcome thi aboon.
We feel sorry for thi bride to be,
And no words con e'er express,
The love thad hoo did feel for thee,
And neaw in deep distress.
And we's aw miss thi, that's for sure,
Wi a love thad never fails,
And though tha's gone through Heaven's door,
The Duck and Trumpet tales
Will still be read bi fooak deawn here,
For sich stories will live on
Bi fooak as howd thi oh so dear,
Tha'll still live, although tha'rt gone.
So goodneet owd brid, lad hev no fear
As wi think of times long past,
Farewell you fine young balladeer,
For eawr thowts for thee will last.

To Bondy

Dave Dutton (Atherton)

There's a dark cleawd that's lyin o'er Lancashire
And t' sky is cowd and grey.
On a misty Autumn morning,
Bondy slipped away…

And someheaw words seem so useless,
Just a waste of a damn good mon.
And a heart filled wi fun and wi laughter.
Wheer is it neaw? It's just gone…

I shake me yed and I wonder.
Just what it's aw abeawt
That roarin greyt fire of talent
Lahk a tuppeny candle's snuffed eawt.

No moor will we hear his 'Accy' twang
Or shake him by the 'ond.
That's it. There's no moor monologues
Or poems by Alan Bond.

But ay what a legacy he's left
You con choose where'er you like.
Ther's poems t' mek yer skrike wi laughter.
An poems t' mek yer skrike.

And they're written in the language
That Bondy loved the best.
Lovingly crafted in Lanky
And in time, they'll stand the test…

For wheerever Lancastrians gather
Fer a crack and one or two beers
Bondy 's poems'll fill em wi laughter
Bondy's poems will fill em wi tears.

Tha's filled us wi' tears owd pal Bondy
'Cos it's hard to accept it's the end.
Thi sweetheart has lost a good husband,
And Lancashire's lost a good friend…
(R.I.P. owd lad…)

SILLY BILLY

I'll tell the tale of Billy Myers,
Always having chip pan fires.
His prowess with a frying pan,
Is just the worst thing known to man.
He never listens to advice-
He's burned his house down (more than twice)
His home with smoke is always filled,
All his meals are charcoal grilled.
The clouds of smoke make Billy cough
He's forgot to turn the chip pan off.
He starts to fry a nice pork chop,
Then goes for fags, down to the shop.
Billy never takes the blame
For tea towels bursting into flame.
He thinks he's done a real good job,
They hang (to dry) above the hob.
Radio, fridge and kettle jug,
Three wires into just one plug.
He thinks it's easier on his pocket,
Everything plugged into just one socket.
As sure as Bill's got half a brain,

He'll set his house on fire again.
Unless like you, Bill reads the word
And fills his chip pan, just one third.
Then stay and watch them, (keep on looking)
Don't watch telly whilst they're cooking.
And when they're golden, (cooked a treat)
Move the pan, turn off the heat.
If the tea towel's wet, to get it dryer,
Hang it where it can't catch fire.
Washer, toaster, micro, use
One plug on each, with proper fuse.
For total safety, (don't you knock it.)
Every plug should have one socket.
So if advice you wish to seek,
Within this Fire Safety Week,
Ring your nearest Fire Brigade,
They'll be pleased to help and aid.
BUT!
If you ignore the things they say,
Like Bill's, your house will burn one day.

BILLY MYERS IS NO ORDINARY BLOKE

Billy Myers is no ordinary bloke,
In fact he once tried knitting smoke
And nearly finished up in gaol,
So listen in, I'll tell the tale.
I'll tell you Billy's tale of woe,
Was Christmas Eve, some years ago,
While celebrating, on a spree,
He'd forgot to buy a Christmas tree.

Shops were shut and locked up tight
And Billy daren't go home that night.
But he had spotted, in the town
A Christmas tree of high renown,
Provided by the mayor (so kind)
And Billy thought they wouldn't mind
If he could climb it (no mean feat)
And pinch the topmost seven feet.

He did just that and homeward brought
The Christmas tree which cost him nought.
He stood on the fairy lights and split 'em
So put some candles on and lit 'em
Now Christmas trees and candles do not mix
This put the Myers in a fix
'Cos while they all were soundly sleeping
Flames up Billy's walls were leaping

Meanwhile!

A policeman saw the tree decapitated
Set off to find the one who'd perpetrated
He saw the needles on the floor
And followed them to Billy's door
What he found there, made him choke
Billy's house was full of smoke.
The fire brigade came double quick
And rescued them in just a tick (hurray)
The PC he was most annoyed
The evidence had been destroyed
The policeman left 'cos he'd been bested.
Billy would not be arrested.
So please take note and hear my plea
Don't put candles on your Christmas tree.

A TRAMP'S STORY

Once I lived in a castle,
With a big moat all around,
A Rolls Royce in the garage,
But, I went and burned it down.

So I moved into a mansion
Where royalty would call,
With a Jaguar in the driveway
But I burned that down an' all

I took a country cottage
With my Ford parked at the door
I lit some party candles,
My cottage is no more.

I got a lovely terraced house,
My motorbike was great.
If hadn't cleaned it with petrol,
I'd still have been there yet.

My prefab and my push bike,
Burned like all the rest.
With clothes left airing by the fire,
My pants and shirt and vest.

Now I'm living very rough,
I sleep in sheds and barns.
I'd still be in my castle
If I'd bought some smoke alarms.

THE SMOKE ALARM THAT GOT A CHRISTMAS PRESENT

I bought a battery smoke detector
For my mother to protect her.
I screwed it to the staircase ceiling
Set off home with wondrous feeling
Done my good deed for the year
From fire, she would have no fear.

It's ages since I fixed it there
But being one with lots of care
I've given it a Christmas present
Not a turkey or roasting pheasant
But plugging in the vacuum cleaner
I got serious and keener.

Then like a Fire Brigade Inspector
I vacuumed mother's smoke detector
I saved my money (didn't do the lottery)
Bought the unit a brand new battery

I'll have the strength, to God I pray
To do that every Christmas Day
So when you're safely home indoors
Do the very same to yours.

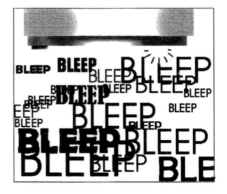